PARTS OF A PLANT

A Look at Stems and Shoots

Lindsey Lowe

KidHaven PUBLISHING

Published in 2020 by
KidHaven Publishing, an Imprint of
Greenhaven Publishing, LLC
353 3rd Avenue
Suite 255
New York, NY 10010

For Brown Bear Books Ltd:
Text and Editor: Lindsey Lowe
Children's Publisher: Anne O'Daly
Design Manager: Keith Davis
Picture Manager: Sophie Mortimer

Picture Credits
t=top, c=center, b=bottom, l=left, r=right

Interior: Dreamstime: Brian Scantlebury 5t; iStock: 20, 21, delectus, 19b, holgs 12, Onfokus 16-17, Studio Light and Shade 17c; Shutterstock: 5b, 6b, 11br, 17br, 17brr, Africa Studio 11bl, Cameilia 8bc, Gan Chaonan 8r, Angel DiBilio 15b, Nick Fox 7b, Sanit fuangnakhon 17bc, Richard Griffin 11bc, Jian Hongyan 16br, Ronnie Howard 13b, Anan Khammul 13t, Lev kropotov 16bl, Oleksandr Lytuyenko 17bl, Jon Manjeot 14r, Meilica 10, B Norris 6-7, NothingIsEverything 11t, patjo 15t, Algars Reinhold 18-19, rootstock 9, Max Topchii 14b, tom Viggins 4, Zieusin 18b.
All other photos and artwork, Brown Bear Books.

Brown Bear Books has made every attempt to contact the copyright holder.
If anyone has any information about omissions please contact licensing@brownbearbooks.co.uk

Cataloging-in-Publication Data

Names: Lowe, Lindsey.
Title: A look at stems and shoots / Lindsey Lowe.
Description: New York : KidHaven Publishing, 2020. | Series: Parts of a plant | Includes glossary and index.
Identifiers: ISBN 9781534533813 (pbk.) | ISBN 9781534533837 (library bound) | ISBN 9781534533820 (6 pack) | ISBN 9781534533844 (ebook)
Subjects: LCSH: Stems (Botany)--Juvenile literature.| Plant anatomy--Juvenile literature.
Classification: LCC QK646.L694 2020 | DDC 581.4'95--dc23

Manufactured in the United States of America

CPSIA Compliance Information: Batch #BW20KL:
For further information contact Greenhaven Publishing LLC, New York, New York at 1-844-317-7404.

Contents

What Are Stems? 4
How Stems Grow 6
Kinds of Stems 8
Underground Stems 10
Stems and Animals 12
How Stems Survive 14
Stems and People 16
Using Tree Stems 18
Grow It! 20
Cook It! 21

Glossary 22
Further Resources 23
Index 24

What Are Stems?

The stem supports the leaves and flowers of a plant. It also carries water and food around the plant so it can grow.

As a plant grows, its stem gets taller and thicker. It is able to support more leaves and flowers. The stem is also the plant's pipeline. There are lots of tiny pipes inside every stem. These carry water and nutrients between the plant's leaves and roots. Most stems grow above the ground. Some plants, like potatoes and onions, have stems that grow under the ground.

THAT'S AMAZING!

A tree trunk is a stem. Every year, the trunk grows in summer and stops growing in winter. This makes rings inside the stem. You can tell how old a tree is by counting the rings!

Plant Pipeline

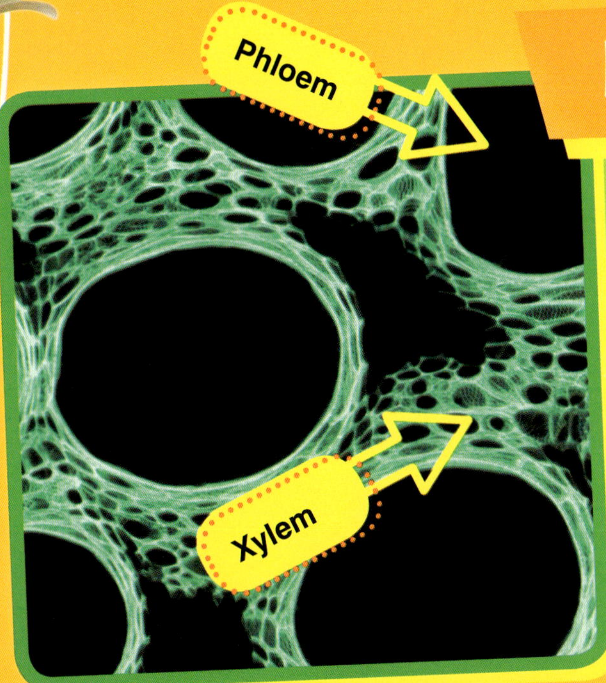

There are two kinds of pipes inside every stem. You can see them through a microscope. Thin pipes called xylem carry water from the roots. Thicker pipes called phloem carry food from the leaves to the rest of the plant.

How Stems Grow

Stems start growing from seeds under the ground. They begin as little green shoots.

The bud at the top of the stem is called the terminal bud. Buds can also grow on the sides of the stem. These lateral buds can grow into new shoots, leaves, or flowers.

Short and Tall

Some stems grow less than one inch (2.5 cm) tall and no thicker than a thread of cotton. But tree trunks can grow hundreds of feet tall. Trees are the tallest living things in the world.

THAT'S AMAZING!

Aspen trees have very long lateral, or sideways, roots. These spread for miles under the ground. New stems called suckers grow up from the lateral roots. Utah's Fishlake National Forest has 47,000 identical aspen trees that have all grown from a single underground root!

Giant Redwood

The biggest stems belong to giant redwood trees. In 2006, a tree named Hyperion was named as the tallest tree in the world. It is 380 feet (116 m). Another large redwood (see right) has a 6-foot (1.8 m) hole cut in it that people can drive through!

Kinds of Stems

Some plants grow a single stem. Others grow a group or clump of stems. Some stems climb or grow along the ground.

Clumps of stems protect the plant from cold winds and hot sun. Plants that have more than one stem do not always grow as tall as plants with single stems. They often grow where they are shaded by other plants. However, some, such as bamboo, can grow very tall.

Strawberries and cucumbers have stems that spread out sideways along the ground. These kinds of stems are called runners or stolons.

THAT'S AMAZING!

Bamboo is the fastest-growing plant on Earth. Some kinds grow up to 35 inches (91 cm) in a single day! The stems grow in clumps, or from stems growing sideways underground.

Climbers

Some plants have a way to grow tall without needing a strong stem or thick trunk. They do this by climbing. Some climbing plants, like beans (see left), have stems that twist around an object. Other climbers have hooks and suckers that help them climb up walls or fences.

Underground Stems

Plants make food in the summer. Some store the food they don't use in thick stems underground.

Plants use underground stems as a way to survive the cold in winter. The stem lies protected in the soil through the winter. In spring, the plant grows new shoots using the food stored in the stem.

Food Stores

There are four kinds of underground stems. A bulb is a rounded stem with layers like an onion. A corm is like a bulb, but without the layers. A tuber is a knobbly, swollen stem. A rhizome is a stem that grows and spreads sideways underground.

Hyacinth Bulb

THAT'S AMAZING!

The layers inside an onion bulb are called scales. Each scale is swollen with stored food. A new plant stem grows from the center of the onion. The heaviest onion in the world was grown in the UK in 2014. It weighed nearly 19 pounds (8.6 kg)!

Potato Tuber

Crocus Corm

Ginger Rhizome

Stems and Animals

Many animals use plant stems to build homes. Other animals use stems for food.

Chimpanzees, orangutans, and gorillas make nests to sleep in every night. Most rodents, such as mice and squirrels, build nests, too. But the best nest builders are birds.

Stems for Nests

Birds lay their eggs and raise their chicks in nests. Stems can be woven into all kinds of different shapes. Storks build huge, flat nests. Small birds twist sticks and stems to make cup-shaped nests. Weaver birds (see right) make large nests that hang upside down from trees.

Stems for Food

Animals that eat stems are called browsers. The biggest browsers are elephants. Old, woody stems are often too tough to eat, so they search out shoots and grass stems. Adult male elephants eat up to 350 pounds (160 kg) of grass or leaves every day.

THAT'S AMAZING!

Beavers gnaw through tree trunks and put them across streams. They put piles of twigs and leaves on top to make dams. Water piles up behind the dam, making a deep pond. The beavers make a nest in the middle of the pond, safely away from predators. The world's biggest beaver dam is 2,790 feet (850 m) wide. It can be seen from space!

How Stems Survive

Most animals eat plants. Some plants have ways to protect their stems from hungry animals.

Oleander plants protect themselves with poison. Nettles have leaves that give a sharp sting. In hot, dry places, juicy plant stems attract thirsty animals. Many desert plants have thorns to keep them away. Honey locust trees have needlelike spines that can grow up to 8 inches (20 cm) long.

Cacti grow in hot, dry deserts. They have prickly spikes on their stems to keep animals away.

Rose Thorns

Roses have colorful flowers to attract insects that will spread their pollen. But most roses have stems with very sharp thorns to keep other animals away.

THAT'S AMAZING!

Mexican acacia trees have an unusual way of protecting themselves. Ants live inside their thorns! The ants get a home and food. They scare away other insects in return. Once a year, they allow bees to collect pollen from the flowers.

Stems and People

People eat the young stems and shoots of many plants. They even use the sap from tree trunks.

Most plant stems are too tough for people to eat, but some are soft and juicy when they are young. Other stems are used to make things people need. Flax stems can be made into linen cloth. Tree bark is used to make cork and aspirin. Rubber, eucalyptus oil, and tea tree oil come from tree sap.

Stem Power

Here are different kinds of stems that people can eat. Bamboo shoots are often used in Chinese cooking. Sugarcane, chopped and boiled in water, makes sugar.

Broccoli

Bamboo Shoot

THAT'S AMAZING!

Maple syrup is the sap of the maple tree. It was first collected by native people in North America, then by European settlers. The sap is boiled to make maple syrup. This tastes good on waffles and pancakes. It also contains minerals such as zinc, calcium, iron, and potassium. These all help to keep us healthy!

Metal pegs are pushed into the maple tree trunk. The watery sap drips out and collects in a bucket.

Parsley

Sugarcane

Potatoes

Asparagus

Using Tree Stems

People have used plant stems to make tools and shelters since ancient times. Wood is still used today.

Early people used thick stems to make ax handles. They used soft stems to make bows. The first shelters and houses were made from woody stems. The remains of the world's oldest house are in Japan. The house was built from sticks 600,000 years ago!

THAT'S AMAZING!

Wood grows in lines called grain. Woodworkers try to follow the natural direction of the wood grain. Most baseball bats are made from ash or maple trees. The bats are made with the straight grain running along the length of the bat. This makes it strong and keeps it from cracking!

Wood and Timber

Wood is a good building material. It is strong and easy to cut and carve. Wood comes from the trunks or stems of trees. Wood used for building is called timber. More than a billion trees are cut down for wood every year. New trees are grown to replace them. Not all timber is used for building. Some wood is crushed and pulped and used to make paper.

Burning Wood

In the early 1900s, 90 percent of Americans burned wood to heat their homes. Today, it is around 1.9 percent. Burning wood for energy harms the environment. However, nearly three billion people worldwide still use wood for cooking and heating.

Grow It!

It's easy to grow crocus plants in pots. When they have finished growing, put the pots in a cold shed or garage for the winter. These are underground stems, so the corm will sprout again in spring!

Here's How

- Fill some pots with fresh, soil-based potting compost. Make sure your pots have good drainage holes at the bottom. If roots sit in water, they will rot.

- Make holes in the compost about 4 inches (10 cm) deep. Plant the corms about 2 to 3 inches (5 to 7.5 cm) apart. Plant them with the points facing up. Leave the tips of the point sticking up slightly above the top of the soil.

- Gently pat the soil around each corm and water them.

- The roots will grow in the fall. If it is very warm, some stems might appear in fall. When buds and flowers appear in the early spring, put the pots in a sunny place and water regularly.

- When the flowers die in the summer, cut off the dead stems and stop watering. Put the pots in a cool place until the following spring.

Cook It!

Asparagus is easy to cook. Try these three ways to enjoy the tasty green stems!

1 large bundle of asparagus, with the woody ends snapped off and thrown away

olive oil

salt, to taste

black pepper

lemon slices (if wanted, to serve)

Here's How

1 **Grilled Asparagus**
Heat a skillet. Toss the asparagus gently in a bowl with a little olive oil. Season with salt and pepper. Grill the stems over a medium heat, turning occasionally, until the stems are tender and browned on all sides. Serve with lemon slices, if using.

2 **Blanched Asparagus**
Bring a large pot of salted water to a boil. Add the asparagus and simmer for about 3 minutes, or until the stems are bright green and tender. Add salt and pepper.

3 **Roasted Asparagus**
Preheat the oven to 400°F (200°C). Toss the asparagus in a little olive oil on a baking sheet. Add salt and pepper. Roast in the oven for about 25 minutes, or until tender and slightly browned.

WARNING
Most cooking involves heating ingredients. Be careful as you cook and make sure an adult kitchen assistant is around to help!

Glossary

browser An animal that feeds on stems, shoots, and leaves.

bud A tip on a stem that grows into a new shoot or flower.

bulb A thick underground stem made from layers called scales.

corm A thick underground stem like a bulb but without layers.

lateral bud A bud that grows on the side of a stem.

phloem The thick pipes that carry food down through a stem.

pollen The powder made by a flower's male parts.

predator An animal that hunts other animals.

rhizome A stem that grows sideways underground.

rodent A small, furry animal with two long front teeth.

sap The sticky juice inside a plant stem.

scales The layers in a bulb.

shoot A new young stem.

terminal bud The bud at the tip or end of a stem.

tuber An underground stem that forms a knobbly lump.

xylem The thin pipes that carry water and chemicals up through a plant stem.

Further Resources

Books

Aloian, Molly. *What Are Stems?* New York: Crabtree Publishing, 2012.

Dickmann, Nancy. *Q & A About Plants* (Curious Nature). New York: Powerkids Press, 2017.

Hansen, Grace. *Stems.* Minneapolis, MN: Abdo Kids, 2016.

Messner, Kate. *Up in the Garden and Down in the Dirt.* San Francisco: Chronicle Books, 2017.

Websites

https://wiki.kidzsearch.com/wiki/Plant_stem

https://scienceprojectideasforkids.com/plant-root-shootsystems/

Index

acacia trees 14, 15
ants 15
asparagus 17, 21

bamboo 8, 9, 16
baseball bats 18
beavers 13
browsers 13
bud 6, 20, 22

cacti 14
climbers 9

ginger 17
grain 18
grass 12

houses 18

maple syrup 17

nests 12, 13

oleanders 14
onion 4, 10, 11

paper 19

redwood tree 7
rhizome 10, 11, 21
roses 15

shoots 6, 13, 16, 22
storks 12
suckers 7, 9
sugarcane 15, 17

thorns 14, 15
tuber 10, 11, 22

weaver birds 12